MIDDLE-CLASS MILLIONAIRE

Middle-Class
Millionaire

FROM $80K IN DEBT TO $3M IN PROFITS
THROUGH CATALYST TRADING

Kyle Dennis

LIONCREST
PUBLISHING

COPYRIGHT © 2018 KYLE DENNIS

MIDDLE-CLASS MILLIONAIRE

From $80K in Debt to $3M in Profits through Catalyst Trading

ISBN 978-1-5445-1016-3 *Hardcover*

       978-1-5445-1017-0 *Paperback*

       978-1-5445-1018-7 *Ebook*

       978-1-5445-1019-4 *Audiobook*

Contents

Introduction

Throughout high school and during my first years in college, I had no experience with stock trading. It's not something they teach kids in school, so like most people, I only knew about it in the vaguest possible terms.

As a result, when I finally got into stock trading, I was way behind the curve and started from scratch. I didn't know much of anything about finances beyond basic life skills. I could write a check, balance my checkbook, and I understood what a mortgage was, but I had no idea what it meant to invest long term. Yet here I am, a few short years after graduating from college, enjoying a wild amount of success beyond anything I ever imagined, as a direct result of trading and investing. How did I get here?

First, to gain a little bit of knowledge about stock trading,

I simply did my homework, listened to financial podcasts, read relevant articles, and learned the basics. I became acquainted with the opinions of knowledgeable people, and I regularly perused the business section of the newspaper, trying to correlate the stuff I read there with how stocks were moving. In all of this, I gained an understanding of the stock market and how it operates, but I still had no idea how to get started trading stocks myself.

I have found that many people are interested in learning how to invest or trade stocks, but they lack the knowledge to get started. Even if they have a basic understanding of how the stock market works, they are unclear about taking that first step. In every line of work, there are people who could benefit from learning how to trade, but they simply need the education that wasn't provided to them in high school or college. They need to know what the opportunities are, how to take advantage of them, and how to get involved.

WHO DO YOU TRUST?

What makes learning in the financial industry difficult is that people don't know who to trust. In the field of stock trading, there are far too many self-appointed experts trying to take advantage of people. Even some of the experts on network TV can't be fully trusted. You have to be a good judge of character in order to identify the people and services that aren't just trying to take your money. You need someone who will speak honestly and provide reliable information, but there's a lot of nonsense and noise out there.

Now that I've achieved success, I want to help and train others to find the success they're hoping for. I fully understand the hesitation people might feel in trusting me (or anybody in this field), because there's such a lack of quality advice. There are too many experts promising huge results and under-delivering on those promises. Maybe you've already been burned. Maybe you've spent a lot of money on books, courses, and webinars only to wind up frustrated.

When I first got started, I looked for experts who didn't push too much, who shared their expertise and information generously. I knew nothing about trading, so I understood how vulnerable I was to scams. If you're in the same boat, I fully relate to how you feel right now. You need to find trustworthy ways to learn and develop skills in investing and trading.

I started by reading books, because I figured if somebody took the time to write, revise, and publish a book, then they must know something. Many famous investors recommend specific books. I intentionally avoided getting my information from the internet or TV because I couldn't verify the information from many of the people sharing through those sources.

Despite my careful approach, I still went through a lot of trial and error to get where I am today. I made mistakes and attempted many wrong things. Most people do the same when they first get started in trading. There are so many obstacles that if you don't know what you're doing, you will find it almost impossible to succeed. The barriers to entry are high, and you have shady people constantly trying to misdirect you—people who aren't looking out for your well-being.

Of course, in my own journey, I did eventually find a few experts that I could trust, and they provided me with solid information. I picked their brains, asked countless questions, and learned from their examples. It made a huge difference.

When I began my website, Biotech Breakouts, and the Nucleus mentorship program, my goal was to become the kind of resource I needed when I was new to this field. I wanted to provide the kind of reliable service and genuine help that would have enabled me to achieve my success much faster. Through Biotech Breakouts, I teach people the specifics of catalyst stock trading. Nucleus is a service for people who want to go even deeper, providing subscribers with real-time access to me throughout the day.

Now more than ever, I want to help you and others like you avoid some of the major obstacles by sharing my own successes and failures. What took me years to learn might take you much less time. That's my hope. Yes, sometimes learning how to navigate the stock market is difficult and frustrating, but with the right person in your corner—someone who truly cares about your success—you can avoid many of the pitfalls.

A CREDIBLE SOURCE

Why should you trust me? You don't even know me! Hopefully, that will change over the course of reading this book.

I was just a normal middle-class kid. I grew up in Los Angeles and had a typical home with a mom, dad, a brother, and a couple of dogs. I went to public school and, after graduating, attended UCLA. Like so many college students, after the grind of earning a degree, I came out of the university with a ton of student loan debt—$80,000 to be precise.

In other words, I didn't start off with a lot of money or any special advantage. As they say, I wasn't born with a silver spoon in my mouth. I did, however, manage to save a little bit of money during college while working as a security guard, but I had no idea how to use that money to create major success.

I did well in college, but I didn't graduate at the top of my class by any means. I'm not a genius. After college, I worked as a real estate analyst, earning a mediocre salary. Still, I was able to save $15,000, which, after five years of stock trading, I turned into $3.1 million. That allowed me to pay off those huge student loans, and as you can imagine, it has changed my life.

Getting to this point didn't happen smoothly. I made a lot of rookie mistakes, even losing half of my account at one point. But I built it back up. I tried many different trading strategies, listened to and learned from many different people, and eventually figured out how to make trading work. To this day, I continue to learn new things.

I don't think anything I've accomplished is unique or even particularly extraordinary. I don't think my success required any special skills or abilities. It was simply a matter of developing discipline and adopting the right strategy. I've proven that taking a small amount of starting capital and turning it into millions can work, and I believe that almost anyone can do the same.

YOUR SUCCESS STORY

I'm fully convinced your success story could be similar to mine. My strategy isn't fancy or overly complex. It's something I've built along the way, as I picked up new techniques and ideas.

What are the keys to making it work? A passion for learning, a lack of ego, a willingness to listen to people who are smarter than you, even a willingness to listen to some people who are less smart than you. There's always something new to learn, especially in trading, because everything changes on a daily basis. If you have the right mindset, if you have dedication and passion, there's no reason why you can't take a small amount of money and turn it into a huge financial success.

Of course, you'll write your own success story. My hope is that this book will help you get started.

In part one, I will provide you with insight into key aspects of financial success. When people hear that I took $15,000 and turned it into $3.1 million within five years, they tend to think of it as an overnight success. That's simply not true. The only overnight success story comes from winning the lottery. Getting where I am now took hard work, passion, and dedication.

I spent a lot of time learning, even though I was already working a nine-to-five job at the time. It wasn't easy, but I made it happen. On the way to work and on the way home, I listened to financial podcasts or audiobooks. If you can't dedicate yourself to learning about this industry, if you're unwilling to carve out the time, you won't find success. Even though my story happened relatively quickly, it still took five solid years until I mastered my strategy. Trust me, it has been a long process of hard work.

In part two, I will provide insight into the mindset and techniques necessary to achieve success in trading. Beyond dedication and passion, beyond reading books and learning, you have to check your ego at the door. In the world of stock trading, ego is a big problem. You have to be able to cut your losses in order to maximize your gains. You have to work methodically and realize that you can be wrong, that some of your decisions will be mistakes. If you can't do that, one bad trade could destroy your account.

I used to play baseball, and I see a lot of similarities between the game of baseball and stock trading. As a baseball player, you don't hit a home run every time you go up to bat. On the contrary, if your batting average is .300, you're doing very well. Stock trading is similar. You're not going to hit every trade out of the park. Instead, you want to go for the singles and doubles. You're doing well if you're right more often than you're wrong, but you can't beat yourself up every time you make a mistake. You learn and move on to the next trade.

In part three, I will provide insight into the personal gains you can achieve if you succeed at this strategy. If you get it right, you can take a small amount of money (like my initial $15,000) and, with relatively few expenses and a lot of freedom, build it into something that could earn you a million dollars a year consistently. Not everyone who reads this book will be able to earn millions, but a few will. There aren't many businesses or industries that provide you with that kind of opportunity.

YOUR JOURNEY IS YOUR BUSINESS

It's important to look at this journey into stock trading as a business. Many people get in trouble because they put too much money into a single risky stock, hoping for wild success, or they take actions without doing enough research. They let emotion determine when they buy and sell, rather than following a consistent strategy or business plan.

Some people approach stock trading like they're playing roulette: they put all of their money on a single risky stock, cross their fingers, and hope for something amazing to happen. That's exactly what I did when I first started. You would never do that in any other area of your life. You wouldn't go out and buy a house without doing research or start a new job without knowing anything about the company. Trading is a business, not a hobby, not a game at a casino, and if you treat it that way, you're setting yourself up for disaster.

It's important to have the right attitude so you understand that you're going to experience occasional losses. When you discover a strategy that works, don't let your emotions run wild. Maintain a methodical approach and just keep making those smart investments.

Personally, I like to develop and write out a business plan for each of my specific trading strategies, just as if I were running any other kind of business. After all, if you wanted to start a business, you'd make a plan, test it out, then implement it. Test the waters. Take it slow. Don't do any anything too fast. Above all, control your emotions.

A level-headed approach will get you a long way. It's not a bad idea to have a full-time job in the beginning so you can take your time, learn, and test your strategies before diving in. Paper trading (trading with a small amount of money) can help you figure out what works. Once you know what you're doing, you can determine whether to go all in—aiming for millions of dollars—or to simply trade stocks as a side income, earning $1,000 to $5,000 a month. If you approach it with the right mindset, you can ramp up your success as you see fit. That's my story, after all, and it can be your story, too.

PART ONE

—

The Untold Story of Trading Success

CHAPTER ONE

Finding Your Inspiration

I attended a small high school in Los Angeles called LACES: Los Angeles Center for Enriched Studies. It's a public university preparatory school located in the Faircrest Heights district. I was always good at math and science—not as good at English and history—and I loved working with numbers. Statistics classes, in particular, were a lot of fun. Trying to predict outcomes in different situations fascinated me.

I was also a big fan of fantasy baseball and basketball, especially making trades and trying to predict which players were going to perform well in the future. This personal interest served me well when I got into the stock market because, in trading, you're always trying to predict which stock will go up and which will go down. I didn't realize this in high school, however. I didn't have any interest in the stock market yet—it never even crossed my mind.

At the same time, I enjoyed watching a medical drama called *House*. You might remember it. Many episodes revolved around the main character, an unconventional doctor named Gregory House, trying to solve difficult medical cases. He identified strange or mysterious symptoms and pieced them together like a puzzle to make a diagnosis. I enjoyed that whole investigative process, so when I went to college at UCLA, I decided that becoming a doctor might be a good career choice for me. Based on the show, it seemed like an interesting job, and it also seemed like a good fit for my personality and preferences. Of course, basing a career decision on a television show is a dumb idea—I realize that in retrospect. But at the time, it made sense.

My favorite TV show wasn't the only deciding factor, of course. My fondness for math and science also seemed like they might be beneficial in the medical field, so I decided to enter college as a biology major with a pre-med indication. I focused all of my effort on becoming a doctor. I took all of the required classes and poured all my energy into the work. I thought I had my future career figured out.

Two years into the program, however, I had a fateful

conversation with my aunt. She had just graduated from medical school and was about to start working full time in the field. When the subject of my future career came up, I was excited to talk to her about it. We had something in common. I expected her to be excited, to congratulate me, and to talk about all of the great experiences I had to look forward to. She didn't do that. Instead, when she talked to me about my chosen career, she strongly emphasized just how difficult it was. She gave me a clear sense of how much work it took to graduate from medical school, and then she told me how much commitment is required to succeed as a doctor.

"I've wanted to become a doctor from the time I was four years old," she said. "That makes all of the hard work worth it to me. But if you don't really have a passion for it, you shouldn't get into this field. It's a ton of work. The pay is good, but for the amount of work you put in and the amount of stress you deal with every day, you're not going to make it unless you have a very strong desire to be a doctor. It has to be your dream in life."

Well, to be honest, I didn't have a strong desire to become a doctor, and it had never been my dream in life. It had just seemed like a good idea, a good fit for my abilities, and an interesting line of work. That conversation with my aunt changed my mind, so I tried to switch my major to biomedical engineering. As it turned out, that degree required taking a bunch of new classes, which would have meant staying in college an extra year and a half. With tuition already over $20,000 a year, I just didn't think I could afford the extra semesters.

Reluctantly, I decided to stick with my biology degree and figure it all out later. In reality, I felt lost. I no longer knew what I wanted to do with my life. I searched online for different careers, but nothing felt right. When I finished my degree and graduated in June of 2012, I still had no idea what I wanted to do long term. Because I needed a job (and had a stressful amount of student loan debt to pay off), I started working as an analyst at a real estate firm out in the Pacific Palisades. A real estate analyst evaluates the market in order to provide statistical data for principal buyers and funds, so it seemed like a fairly good fit with my mathematical abilities.

Nevertheless, the real estate job was intended to be temporary. I still wanted to do something with my biology degree, but I had no idea what that might be. I briefly considered entering the field of forensics, where I could use my knowledge of biology and my investigative mind to help solve crimes like the people on CSI. Ultimately, however, I decided to become a certified EMT. I took a three-month course to earn my certification and started going out in an ambulance part time, primarily performing CPR. My long-term goal was to become a firefighter since it seemed to have the best long-term prospects. In the meantime, I kept my full-time job as a real estate analyst.

At the time, Los Angeles had a hiring freeze on firefighters that had gone on for five or six years. When it ended, the city organized a job fair at the LA Convention Center. Thirty thousand people showed up to take a test in order to become firefighters, but only a hundred jobs were available. Many of them came from an EMT background. I knew I was way underqualified compared to most of the people there—some of those EMTs and paramedics had been on the job for years. I wasn't all that surprised when I didn't get the job.

Failing to become a firefighter, I continued my work in real estate, but I still felt utterly adrift. During college, I had read a few books and listened to some podcasts on stock trading. At the time, I'd thought it was good information to have in case I wanted to invest my money once I obtained a career; I didn't want to simply give the money to a financial advisor.

One of the books I read was *The Intelligent Investor* by Benjamin Graham, a book that Warren Buffet has credited in interviews for changing his life and putting him on the path to success. I also read books on technical analysis of the stock market. All of this learning made me develop a bit of interest in the market, but I had no intention of becoming a professional investor or trader.

In reality, I came to enjoy my work at the real estate firm—it involved a lot of number crunching, which was right up my alley. However, the structure of the job didn't work for me. I arrived at 8 a.m., left at 5 p.m., and did the same work every single day. Although it was interesting, it wasn't my passion. I felt dissatisfied with my direction in life. I was searching, and that's what ultimately led me to stock trading. I know this is something many young people go through after college. Maybe you're at that point in your life right now.

WHO ARE YOU?

People tend to get interested in trading for several reasons. They like the idea of being able to work from a computer at home, they want to become their own boss, and they also tend to be frustrated with their current line of work. When I first started, I just wanted to make a bit of extra money. I was dissatisfied with my job, but I didn't yet intend to leave. I think that's true of many people when they first start trading. That might be your situation. Maybe you're just interested in a making a little more money through trading, and you have no intention of making this a full-time profession. Maybe you just want to create a nest egg for yourself.

I know many people who trade part-time while still working other jobs, or they're retired and just need a little extra money. Whatever your situation, if you're willing to put in the hard work, listen, and learn, then you're well on your way to achieving your goals, both financially and in terms of personal satisfaction.

There are many different types of stock trading to choose from, and there's bound to be one that suits your preferences, availability, and skills, so knowing who you are when you get started is important. For example, I know that I prefer short-term, fast-moving trading to the slower moving stocks, because those bore me. If you know yourself, have a clear sense of your own preferences, availability, and skills, it will help you develop a trading strategy that fits your personality and timeframe. Even though I prefer faster-moving stocks, I knew I didn't have time to sit in front of my computer and watch trades all day long. I had another full-time job taking up most of my time. Realizing that, I got involved in something called catalyst trading, which involves putting a month-long hold on stocks that tend to fluctuate wildly from day to day.

On the other hand, some people I talk to dislike stocks that move up and down a lot in a day—it gives them anxiety. They prefer to put on a trade and then go to the garden and relax. I understand that. It's why knowing yourself is so important in developing your strategy.

To figure out the best approach, ask yourself a few questions.

WHAT ARE YOUR PRACTICAL NEEDS?

Identify your goals early on so you know what you need to get out of trading. My biggest practical need was my student loan debt—I needed to pay off $80,000. For you, it might be a mortgage or car payments. Whatever the case, having a clear sense of your own practical needs will provide important motivation to do the hard work. Every time I didn't want to get up early and go make trades, I thought about the student loan debt looming over me.

WHAT DO YOU WANT TO GET OUT OF TRADING IN THE LONG TERM?

Five or ten years from now, what do you hope to accomplish through trading or investing? For me, once I got out of debt, I began to see the real potential in trading. I started dreaming about running my own trading business. I wanted to feel the responsibility and gain the reward of controlling my future so my successes and failures would be determined by how much work I put in. Even if I'd been able to make the same amount of money working as a real estate analyst, I would still have chosen trading because it's so much more rewarding. As a real estate analyst, I monitored market conditions and provided investment advice, and I got paid the same hourly wage no matter how hard I worked. As a stock trader, the harder I work, the more I make. The more I put in, the more I get out. I like that motivation.

I could have become a real estate agent instead of an analyst. My hard work would have paid off then, but I prefer the lifestyle of a stock trader. I like to travel, eat good food, and visit interesting places. Being a professional trader allows me to do all of that. My schedule is highly flexible and firmly in my control. This also provides motivation to keep working hard every day.

PERSEVERANCE AND HARD WORK

Let me be blunt: trading is a hard business. Not everyone will find success with it, but it's possible for anyone to find success if they do the work. Of course, that's true in many businesses, and in life generally. When you put in the hard work, you see the return. However, the hard work of trading creates a big barrier of entry for many people. They get excited about trading, they set big goals, they dream of making a million dollars, but they don't ultimately get anywhere because they don't persevere through the lows that come with the highs.

Many people who join my Nucleus mentorship service aren't actually interested in learning. The goal of my program is to provide resources and advice to help people achieve long-term success at trading. However, many people just want to know which stock is going to go from five to five hundred. They want hot stock tips, and that's not the way to success—that's gambling. Success comes from persevering, learning, and putting in the hard work. If you do that, you will eventually see the dividends.

As you start to achieve success, you will gain confidence. It's a great feeling to sit down at the computer every day and pull profit out of the market over and over again. It's liberating, and—quite frankly—it's a lot of fun. My hope is that I can help you develop the confidence you need so that you, too, can have this experience. I am firmly convinced that a better life is waiting for you, but to get there, you will have to learn how to deal with failure. Success in trading involves a lot of trial and error, so mistakes are inevitable. In the next chapter, we'll look at how to navigate your failures so you can keep moving forward.

CHAPTER TWO

Persevering through Failure

When I first got started in stock trading, I approached it like many first-time traders do: I just tried things out. My goal was to make enough money to pay off my student loans after graduation, save a little bit of money, and set myself up for a prosperous future.

Toward the end of my college career, I tried to get a head start on paying off my student loans, with little success. As I mentioned before, I had read some books on stock trading, so during my senior year, I decided to place a couple of trades. I picked two stocks, both of which were very cheap. That made them seem like a safe entry point. Looking back, I realize now that I shouldn't have been anywhere near those kinds of stocks, but at the time, I figured I could make trades and give it a shot. What did I have to lose? In the end, one of the stocks did decently, giving a 30 percent return, while the other one went bankrupt and doesn't even exist anymore. Together, the return amounted to a little less than nothing.

After graduating from UCLA, I got that job as a real estate acquisitions analyst. During my first six months on the job, I only made $11.25 an hour working part time. After that, they offered me a full-time position, with an annual salary of about $35,000, which doesn't get you very far in Los Angeles. I took the raise, but in order to make ends meet, I decided to move in with my parents. It was the only way I could afford to live on that salary.

I enjoyed my real estate job, but as I said, I didn't feel any real passion for it. It allowed me to do a lot of number crunching and analysis, both of which I'd always been good at; however, the work moved slowly. I spent most of my time entering those numbers into Excel spreadsheets. It didn't have any of the intensity or the immediate return of stock trading.

When I began trading stocks again, I continued working my full-time job, which made for some very long days. On the West Coast, the stock market opens at 6:30 a.m., so I would set my alarm for 5:00 a.m., drive to the office, and sit down at my computer by 6:15 a.m. Then I would get online and trade stocks until 8:30 a.m. After that, I'd work my normal, eight-hour shift, crunching numbers all day. Then I'd come home and read articles and books, research specific stocks, and look at market conditions. Though it was an exhausting schedule, I kept it up for about three years, until October of 2015.

The real estate company liked me, and I was doing a good job. However, they could tell that, increasingly, my heart wasn't in it. Finally, my supervisor sat me down and had a talk with me. Trading had become my true passion, and that was obvious to my coworkers.

"You need to put in a bit more effort and show more passion in your work," he said. "We want to give you a raise, but you have to be more focused."

At that point, I had a choice to make. Either I could stay at the real estate job and keep up the salary grind that I'd been doing for three years, or I could quit and start trading full time. The choice seemed obvious to me, even though the risk made me nervous. I tendered my resignation, and my boss wasn't particularly surprised. Everyone at the company had realized that any time I spoke with enthusiasm, it was always about stock trading—never about real estate analysis.

After quitting, I went out and bought a plastic table and

a couple of computers to put in my living room, and I started trading at home. Looking back at my real estate career, I think I should have left a lot sooner, because I could have started working toward my real success earlier. Still, despite the time constraints, during my three years at the real estate job, I made $500,000 from trading.

When I tell people I made half a million dollars in three years while also working a full-time job, they often tell me that my success seems to have come suddenly. The truth is, getting to that point took a lot of time and effort, and I stumbled into many of the common pitfalls along the way.

After my disappointing attempt at stock trading in college, what made the difference during those three years? I think it was perseverance. I learned to persevere by grinding every day—getting up at five in the morning, trading and working all day, then fighting the LA traffic all the way back home, only to spend my evening researching the stock market. I felt exhausted most of the time, so it required strengthening my mental fortitude just to keep plugging away. My willingness to do that during those three years created a faster track to stock market success when I finally quit real estate and started trading full time.

SWINGING FOR THE FENCES

When I first starting trading, I ran into a lot of problems.

I wanted the gains to come right away. I dreamed of hitting the jackpot and becoming wealthy overnight. Many people think that way when they first start trading. When the money didn't come fast enough, I decided to ramp up the speed of my returns by trading options. This is a very risky way to invest, especially for people who don't know what they're doing. I started with VXX (S&P 500 VIX), which is an exchange-traded note that tracks volatility in the market.

These days, I don't trade VXX very often, and when I do, it's always a very small position. Back then, however, I was putting way too much of my account into VXX options, fingers crossed as I tried to hit home runs. Unfortunately, I lost about $8,000 (about half my account at the time) trying to hit those home runs. It was the biggest catastrophe of my entire career.

I remember one evening, not long after I'd lost the money, lying in my bed at my parents' house and staring at the ceiling, riddled with anxiety.

What in the world am I doing? I thought. *I really messed up. I'll never get that much money back.*

I didn't want to tell my parents or friends that I'd lost a ton of money. I considered cutting my losses and moving on. It seemed like the smarter option. Maybe stock trading wasn't for me. Maybe I didn't have what it took to succeed.

Ultimately, I couldn't walk away. Instead of quitting, I told myself that I was going to battle back, somehow earn that money again, and keep pushing to success. Still, a loss of that size scared me, and I felt embarrassed at the possibility of losing the rest of my money. If that had happened, I would never have been able to pay off my student loans. I might have been in debt for the rest of my life.

Even when I lost money, I enjoyed the process of trading, and I believe it was the sheer enjoyment that kept me in the game during the low point. Instead of cutting my losses, I stepped back and reevaluated my approach. It was clear that I'd gone down the wrong path. Instead of trying to hit home runs with every trade, I needed to focus on the singles and doubles. I needed to adopt a methodical approach, accumulating smaller wins over a longer period of time. To do that, I had to carefully define a strategy rather than making rash trades.

VALUABLE MISTAKES

Once I figured out that strategy, things started to turn around. Making smarter trades, being patient and persistent, I did ultimately earn back that $8,000, and then some. Since then, I've had tremendous success in the stock market. If my story makes anything clear, it's that perseverance pays off. Hanging in there, making smart decisions instead of trying to knock it out of the park with a wild swing, makes all the difference.

I have experienced all of the pitfalls and hard times that most people go through in stock trading, but I never gave up. Beyond simply hanging in there, I devoted the time to learn and improve my strategy. When I worked at the real estate company, it wasn't easy to do research at night, but I knew I needed to do it.

The overwhelming majority of novice stock traders have another full-time job, are just out of college, and want to make more money on the side. However, most of them don't put enough time into learning the best strategies. Even if you're tired in the evenings, you simply have to carve out extra time to learn how to play this game. You're going to have to make sacrifices for the first few years. There's no way around it. That's hard, especially when you also have a job and a family, but it pays off in the long run. Make the sacrifices now so you can enjoy the windfall later. Trust me—you won't regret it.

In the beginning, you'll make a lot of mistakes, just like I did. You have to persevere through those mistakes. Remember, in any business, there are bound to be a few bumps and bruises along the way. You might lose a significant amount of money when you first start trading stocks because you won't know exactly what you're doing. Allow yourself to make those mistakes. Don't be too hard on yourself. If you're willing to keep learning, every mistake will help you perfect your strategy. You can bounce back.

Even large, successful companies like Uber and Tesla struggle and stumble along the way. Uber continues to lose money every year, as does Tesla. How can they be considered successful if they're not turning a profit? Because neither Uber nor Tesla are working toward quick profits. Instead, they are building for the future, focusing on long-term goals that will pay off tremendously. Think of your trading strategy the same way. You must persevere through the hard times, accepting some losses and learning from your mistakes as you hone your strategy, working toward bigger goals in the future.

You're bound to make some bad trades, especially in the beginning, so when it happens, don't take it too hard. Having said that, I believe the principles I share in this book—keeping a level head, keeping your emotions in check, learning from both your losses and your wins—will put you way ahead of the game. Many people let their emotions get the best of them. Of course, every person has emotions, so they're always a factor in trading. However, your decisions must be tempered by a careful strategy.

To be a success in the stock market, you have to pay your dues. I don't know any successful investor who hasn't weathered rough times. When I started, I was happy that I had saved a small amount of money in college. It wasn't much, but it got me started. It's good that I started small, because it meant that when I later lost half of my account, it didn't crush my confidence. I knew I could learn from the loss, take what money was left over, and build it up again. If I'd started with a large amount of money and then lost half of it, it might have discouraged me enough to make me quit. Starting small has its advantages. It makes it easier to learn from the loss and move on.

Even now, when I make a bad trade, my goal is to learn what I did wrong, determine how to improve, and move on. Just know that at every stage of the game, you'll make winning trades and you'll make losing trades. It's part of the business. As long as you control your emotions and learn, you'll continue to grow and become more successful. Learning is the hard part, but it helps to have a strong work ethic.

CHAPTER THREE

Consistent Hard Work

I learned the importance of hard work from my parents, Laurie and Steve, who have both worked incredibly hard their entire lives. My mother started working at sixteen, taking a job as a cashier at a convenience store at Six Flags Magic Mountain, an amusement park in Valencia, California. Fairly quickly, she was promoted to manager of the store, then later became manager of the employee cafeteria. This set an example, climbing the ladder through hard work and dedication. She was always on time, always treated coworkers with respect, and gave her full effort to every task. Those traits have stayed with her, and I observed them growing up.

My mother hasn't had many job interviews in her life, primarily because she hasn't had to. Her reputation precedes her. The various jobs she's held over the years have come through the recommendations of previous employers. For example, she worked as an accountant at a legal firm, and when the lawyer finally retired, he recommended her to a real estate firm—the same real estate firm I worked for after college. She has never left a job in haste. In fact, she has been with her current employer for almost twenty years now. This is all the more impressive because she was the firm's first outside hire, and she still works just as hard every day as she did on day one. Her hard work has paid off at every job, giving her favor with supervisors and enabling her to advance. She taught me to do the same thing, and it has served me well.

My dad worked just as hard. He currently manages his own carpentry company, making everything from birdhouses to potting benches. Prior to that, he worked as a general contractor, where his work consisted of laying tile, installing doors, and about a hundred other things. He became known in the neighborhood for his quality craftsmanship and reliability. All the while, he used his off time to coach my little league baseball teams.

Growing up, I was constantly exposed to the work ethic of my parents, and I also saw, through their example, how hard work pays off. Consequently, I have always tried to put my best effort into anything I do. When I worked at the real estate firm, even though I didn't have a passion for the job, I still worked as hard as I could. Once I started applying that work ethic to stock trading, although I stumbled occasionally in the beginning, it ultimately paid off massively. The effort that I put into trading has a direct impact on what I get out of it.

UNLIKELY MENTORS

In 2011, when I was still a junior in college, I began my first investigation into the stock market by reading books on the subject, books like *Technical Analysis of the Financial Markets* by John J. Murphy, and I followed that up with two books Warren Buffett recommends: *Security Analysis* and *The Intelligent Investor* by Benjamin Graham. There are many, many books that the experts recommend when you start investing, but these three are the ones I happened to pick up. Reading them provided my first understanding of how the market works because, prior to that, I knew absolutely nothing. In fact, the only thing I knew for sure about stock trading was that I would have to put in a ton of hard work to get up to speed with everybody else if I wanted a piece of the pie.

After reading those books, I opened my first trading account in 2012, shortly before my graduation. I went with an online brokerage called TradeKing (which is now called Ally Invest) because they had a very low commission rate.

A friend of mine who had been dabbling in the markets also used TradeKing, so I contacted him for help while setting up my account. He became my first mentor in a long series of mentors. I asked him countless questions about how the market worked, how the platform worked, and how to place trades. He didn't know much beyond the most basic concepts at the time, but he was the only personal resource I had, and all of the online resources were so dense with information that they confused me.

Looking back now, my initial trades seem woefully ill-advised. As I mentioned earlier, I made a couple of investments in cheap stocks and got nothing in return. However, those early trades at least gave me an idea of how the process works, how trades go up and down, and how to follow industry news.

After I graduated and started working at the real estate firm, I got more active in trading, although it was nothing compared to what I do now. The CEO of the real estate firm had a friend who was a professional day trader. The real estate firm rented the floor of a large office building, but since the company didn't have enough people to rent out every room on the floor, the CEO let his friend use one of the offices.

That proved to be fortunate for me because it meant I had an expert I could approach with my questions. In fact, the CEO's friend became another mentor to me, and his office was right across from mine. Whenever I had a question or concern, I picked his brain, and he was generous in sharing what he knew. Over time, we became good friends. He'd been trading since the early 1980s, so he knew significantly more than I did. His willingness to share what he knew helped me immensely in building my trading knowledge, and it's partly what inspires me to share my knowledge these days. I enjoy guiding others the way he guided me, helping them navigate the early stages of stock trading so they can enjoy success down the road.

Even though, as I said, I felt exhausted almost every day, I don't regret the amount of time I put into stock trading during my years at the real estate firm. Days were long and exhausting, and sometimes I was tempted to just come home and crash. However, my drive and determination wouldn't let me do that, so I gave trading all of the time my schedule would permit. I battled traffic for up to an hour every morning to get to work early in the Palisades, just so I could talk to my day trader friend for a while before my normal shift began. After work, I went to the gym, then came home and spent hours reading and researching.

Any time I was in my car, I switched from music stations to financial podcasts. I didn't want to waste any time that I could use to learn more about trading. To this day, I listen almost exclusively to financial podcasts. Putting in all of that extra time to learn wasn't easy, but I don't regret it for one minute. I knew, even back then, that someday, somehow, it would pay off, and it has. If you want to become successful at stock trading, put in the time and effort to learn. Cut out some superfluous activity. Wake up an hour earlier. Do whatever you have to do. It will pay off eventually.

My dad used to listen radio shows about history. As a kid, I always found this weird. I preferred listening to music, and I thought his history shows and talk shows sounded incredibly boring. Now, here I am, fifteen years later, listening to boring podcasts all the time. It's funny how things come full circle. The habits we learn from our parents wind up becoming our own habits, and in my case, it has served me well. However, of all the habits I learned, a strong work ethic has been, by far, the most important.

NINETY PERCENT OF INVESTORS FAIL

Investing in the stock market is one of the most competitive activities you can get involved in. Anything that has this much lucrative potential is going to be intense. If you look at Forbes's list of the wealthiest people, a large percentage of them are investors, and some of the most profitable corporations in the world are investment banks. When you enter this industry, you're competing against the smartest, richest, most powerful people in the world.

You aren't competing with them directly, of course. There's enough money to go around. My point is, if you want to succeed, you're going to have to put in a lot of hard work, but if you're willing to do that, you just might reap huge rewards. Don't come into this business expecting to have everything handed to you. Be prepared to commit a huge amount of time and effort. If you'll do that, and if you'll weather the early stages, there's a light at the end of the tunnel.

Can you put up with the daily grind of investing? That's a question only you can answer. For me, that grind meant getting up very early so I could trade at the opening of the market. All told, between real estate and trading, I was routinely working eleven-hour days. There were times I didn't want to do it, days when I didn't feel good, or when I wanted more sleep. However, I knew that consistency was important. If you want trading to pay off, you have to keep working at it day after day for years.

Are you willing to go above and beyond in order to learn the ropes? Plenty of people work nine-to-five or eight-to-five jobs, but are you willing to work from six in the morning to six in the evening? You need those extra hours to focus on the market, especially if you want to hold on to your full-time job while becoming a successful trader.

A common saying in this industry is, "Ninety percent of

people fail in the stock market." Although that sounds high, I think it's not a bad ratio when you consider the potential for massive profitability. Ten percent of the people who get into trading are enjoying a windfall. That's not too bad. As for the 90 percent who fail, it's mostly because they aren't willing to put in the extra time to research and learn. Even when they try, they often find a lack of good, easy-to-understand resources that teach people the right way to get into the stock market. Sometimes, they're listening to all the wrong people and getting bad advice from shady so-called experts.

Despite the obstacles that lie in front of you, it's quite possible that you might be in that 10 percent. In fact, there's nothing preventing it. The people I've met who are successful in the stock market always have a hardworking mindset. They treat learning about the stock market like working toward a college degree: they know it will take several years of consistent effort to master it. Success is attainable for just about anyone. Believe that and commit to doing whatever it takes to make it happen.

If you enjoy reading books, spend some extra time every day reading about trading. If, like me, you prefer podcasts, find a few good financial podcasts and listen to them regularly. Choose whichever medium works best for you and commit to learning from it. Let successful traders inspire you to change your life, because one day, you'll turn a corner and realize stock trading isn't as hard as it seemed. You'll see that you just needed to spend a little extra time learning.

PART TWO

The Action Steps for Trading Success

CHAPTER FOUR

Treat Trading as Your Business

When I was seven years old, my mother took me to Wells Fargo and opened an account for me with $100. This inspired a lifelong love of saving money. Even as a child, any time my parents gave me money for doing chores, I preferred to save it rather than spend it.

I loved the idea of saving up in order to buy something really expensive. I always found that process exciting. For example, in 1999, Dell came out with a new computer, and I saved up enough to buy one. Since I'd learned to save money at a young age, I knew I would never have trouble doing so as an adult, as long as I had a good job.

On the other hand, I was also motivated to save money

partly out of fear. I had the misfortune of graduating high school in 2008, right when the financial crisis hit. From listening to the news and reading stories, I came to the conclusion that banks and financial advisors either didn't have an investor's best interests in mind or, worse, were totally corrupt. After all, hadn't they caused the financial crisis and hurt a lot of people as a result?

Watching the financial crisis unfold through the media during those formative years made me want to take ownership of my finances. I didn't want anyone else's bad decisions or corrupt practices to destroy my future, so I decided not to let anyone else make financial decisions for me. I still had a bit of money that I'd saved throughout my childhood, and I added to it during college. Eventually, I wanted to invest it in a smart way, but whether I succeeded or failed, I wanted the responsibility to be solely on me.

Though I knew that I wanted to take ownership of my finances, I also knew that ownership alone wasn't enough. I lacked experience to make wise investment decisions, and I didn't have any mentors or experienced family members I could talk to about investing. No one in my family had any working knowledge of the stock market. My grandfather was an engineer, my grandmother an administrator at a school—neither of them had done any stock trading. My mom was an accountant, so she was good with numbers, but she didn't know much about stock market investing. Ultimately, I had to start from scratch.

Because of this lack of mentors and experience, I made a lot of rookie mistakes. I'm not alone in this. You'll probably make some mistakes, too, when you first start trading. It's easy to make rash or ill-informed decisions when you see so much potential for profit in all the stories of successful people on social media, in books, and on television.

As you first start to learn, it can be easy to assume you know more than you really do. What makes the stock market so tricky for beginners is that there's no barrier to entry. Even if you know nothing at all, you can open an account and start trading the very next day with whatever money you have in the bank. That makes it easy to get off on the wrong foot, which is exactly what happened to me. Bear in mind, I moved slowly when I first got started, unlike some people who dive in fully, but I still wound up making mistakes.

BUSINESS, NOT BLACKJACK

Trading in the stock market feels exciting as soon as you get started. You sense the potential right away, and if things start going well, then wild success can seem imminent. However, every trader experiences high points and low points in their trading history, both financially and emotionally.

The key moment in your development as a trader occurs when you hit a low point. If you can identify the problem that got you there, analyze your own strategy, and figure out what you did wrong, then you can turn things around. Sadly, many people reach their low point and give up because it's such an emotional roller coaster. When I hit my low point, it helped me gain perspective on my situation by looking past the emotional roller coaster in order to see stock trading as a business. Just like a business, I saw that I simply needed to develop and adjust my business plan for each trade.

If you approach trading like a business, then you accept that you'll have some losses along the way. Just like a business, you have to test out different strategies to discover what works, and you have to avoid taking unnecessary risks. With a business-oriented mindset, your trading becomes less about following your emotions—what feels right—and more about executing effective strategies and plans that actually work.

My early mistakes helped me realize this. The mindset for success in stock trading is no different than if you're opening a real estate firm or ice cream shop. With any business, you don't simply dive in, open your shop, cross your fingers, and hope for the best. Instead, you crunch the numbers, create a plan, and take a methodical approach. In stock trading, your strategy must be both methodical and repeatable.

Most people who start trading treat it like blackjack. They come in with $2,000, and they want to turn it into $20,000 on their first trade. That mentality might be just fine when you visit a casino in Vegas, but it doesn't work in the stock market. In fact, if you have that risk-taking mentality, you're better off taking that $2,000 and heading to the blackjack table at the nearest casino rather than investing it into some risky stock options, because your odds are much greater. Among casino games, blackjack odds are as close to 50 percent against the house as you can get. With a risky stock trade, you're looking at odds much closer to 5 percent.

When people get into the stock market hoping to hit big right away, then tend to start off very aggressively. It's that kind of behavior that has given stock trading the reputation of being like gambling. Many people on the outside see it as a business of pure chance, where traders are investing blindly and have no control over what happens. That's only true if you enter the market and trade in stock you don't understand, if you fail to do research, or don't develop an effective business plan. In other words, it's only gambling if you treat it like gambling, but the same is true of any business. If you open up an ice cream shop with no plan and no idea what you're doing, it's the same as pulling a lever on a slot machine: maybe you'll hit it big, but most likely you won't.

If you came to this book with a blackjack mindset, your

first and most important step is to start thinking of the stock market differently. I didn't experience any real success until I stopped looking at trading as a way to go from $2,000 to $20,000 overnight. I realized that the real path to success was stacking up wins, bit by bit, to build up my portfolio methodically over time. Once I embraced that approach, I started to achieve real success.

The good news is that executing a trading business plan is much easier than gambling on an unlikely result. Once you find a strategy that works for you and your personality, within your desired timeframe, you can continue refining it to make it even more effective. If you're methodical and precise, your chance of hitting good trades will continue to increase, which will enable you to adopt other investing techniques that will expand your portfolio even more.

OPTIONS AREN'T AN OPTION FOR YOU

Looking back, my rookie mistakes seem exceptionally dumb, but at the time, they made sense to me. Of the two companies I first invested in, one was a pink sheet company, and the other was over the counter (OTC). Both pink sheet and OTC companies are largely unregulated and incredibly risky, unlike the Nasdaq and the NYSE. You might be familiar with them if you've seen the movie *Wolf of Wall Street*, in which Leonardo DiCaprio's character,

Jordan Belfort, pedals pink sheet penny stocks for large commissions. Those are the kinds of stocks I bought.

The first company I bought stock in created metal detectors to help airports detect bombs. The other was a biotech company that sold a pain-relief patch that attached to the inside of a patient's cheek. I made a little bit of money on one of the trades, but the other trade went to zero before I got out. Ultimately, both companies went out of business. Even though I didn't lose a ton of money on those initial investments, I was playing a dangerous game, and I'm lucky it didn't turn out much worse for me. I had absolutely no idea what I was doing.

I followed this unfortunate decision by doing something even riskier: I got into options. Many people don't understand how investing in stock options works. Basically, an options contract allows you to bet on whether or not a specific stock will go up or down within a certain period of time. To be more precise, an options contract gives a buyer the right (but not the obligation) to purchase a stock at a known price in a predefined timeframe by putting down a smaller amount of money up front. That means you can theoretically control a hundred shares for the price of one. If the value of the stock rises during the agreed-upon timeframe, then you still buy it at the agreed-upon price, making a lot of money in the process. You're controlling a much larger position than if you bought the shares directly. In order to profit, the stock has to rise above the price you've set within that timeframe, and that creates the inherent risk.

Since my account was small at the time, I thought investing in options would allow me to use less money in order to control the position of more shares. Even though I had read a book on the subject, I didn't approach options with enough caution, putting 30, 40, even 50 percent of my account into individual positions. I was essentially gambling that the market would take a dramatic turn and give me huge returns. What I didn't know was that those option positions decay each and every day—that they lose value and have an expiration date.

With stocks, you might see your position move 10 percent with a few weeks, but with options, you can see much higher returns, sometimes closer to 100 percent. These dramatic swings are what attract people with smaller accounts, because even with a small account, you have a chance to hit big. This seems easier than grinding out those smaller wins. The danger with options is that you have to be right on two factors: the timeframe during which the stock will go up and how much it will go up.

If a stock is worth $30, when you buy an option, you might decide that the stock will go to $31 within two weeks. When you outright own the shares, you don't have to worry about the timeframe. The stock can go from $30 to $31 in two weeks or two months, and it generally doesn't matter to you. With an option, however, if it doesn't make the move in the specified timeframe, you lose out on whatever you paid for it upfront, all because you didn't time it right.

As you can imagine, options are hard to learn and perfect. These days, I don't trade them very often because I realize now that the way they're constructed is not conducive to making reliable bets. Complicated option strategies can reliably make you money, but they are just that—complicated.

Another risky trade I made in the beginning was getting into VXX, which is an exchange-traded note (ETN) that tracks short-term futures. To put it another way, VXX tracks volatility and fear in the markets. VXX is also constructed with options and futures contracts built into it, so the actual shares decay every day. Not only did I invest in VXX, but I also took options on the VXX stocks, which means I was betting on the decay of the decay. I didn't even know what that meant at the time. Every time the market went up just slightly, my fear-in-the-market indicator went down, and my options went down, as well. At the time, I had no idea what any of these movements meant, which is a sure sign I had no business getting into this kind of investing.

Instead of wasting money on these kinds of risky options,

I should have done just the opposite. I should have started by trading the least risky stocks I could find: highly regulated stocks on the Nasdaq and New York Stock Exchange. Even some Nasdaq stocks are priced low and could be risky if you don't know what you're doing, but they're still far safer than buying options, OTC and pink sheet stocks, or getting into VXX.

I understand why people want to take huge risks like I did. Bigger risks usually have higher potential yields, but your success rate is always much lower. I've seen many people destroy their accounts by trading options and pink sheet stocks. Even if they hit one good winner, it only encourages them to make bigger and bigger bets until they wind up losing all their money. My advice to beginners is to stay away from all risky investment options until you have a better idea of what you're doing and which strategies minimize the risks. Of course, by the time you have that knowledge, you might decide you still don't want to invest in them, and that's not a bad strategy either.

COMPETITORS AND MENTORS

Stock trading involves a lot of competition. Every day, you're competing against other people in the market. There's a winner and loser every second. Every share you buy is a share someone else sold. Every share you sell is a share someone else wants to buy. Some people go long on a stock, while others go short on the same stock, betting it will go down. Every single day, countless people are speculating on every single stock and whether it will go up or down, and in order to be successful, you have to be better than them.

Being better than your competition is more difficult than it sounds. There's a lot of money behind the stock market, and a lot of people wanting a bigger slice of the pie. You don't have to be the richest or the smartest, but you do have to be more knowledgeable and more passionate than the average person. You also need a business strategy and an ability to keep your emotions from getting the best of you. This can be hard in the beginning. If someone brand new to the market went head-to-head against me in trading, I would easily win due to my experience and knowledge. It sounds unfair, but that's the reality of the situation. It's a bit like getting thrown into a shark tank: you'd better be ready to fend for yourself. The first day you step into stock trading, you're up against a bunch of people who know a whole lot more than you.

You best bet is to take things slow and treat trading as a learning process. Don't rush out, like so many people, and just start buying over-the-counter stocks. Expect small returns and aim for consistency. Once you acquire more knowledge and experience than the average trader, you'll be able to extract a lot more money out of the markets. Until then, move slowly and tread carefully.

After making a few early, rash decisions, I had to admit to myself that I didn't know as much about stock trading as I'd thought. That's when I started talking to knowledgeable people and asking questions. As I mentioned earlier, I spent a lot of time picking the brain of the professional trader who worked in the same office as my real estate firm. Having someone that I could speak to directly like that was invaluable. He had traded through a variety of banks since the 1980s, but by the time I met him, he was trading on his own, using nothing but the computer at his desk.

He taught me how stocks are constructed, how different kinds of trades work, and the strategies that he had implemented successfully. I trade in a different way than he did, but learning his strategy helped me to figure out my own. He showed me the ropes and helped me learn faster.

During that time period, I also reached out to various experts online, including Jason Bond. I had an open mind, so I wanted to learn different techniques from various people, even if I didn't end up using those techniques myself. For example, when I first discovered Jason Bond, I was doing a lot of catalyst trading in the biotech sector. That involved looking at various data events—such as drug release dates—that provided stimuli to initiate trades.

Jason, on the other hand, used a variety of technical and mathematical indicators to determine which trades to make, an approach I've never used. However, instead of shunning his advice because it was different from what I practiced, I picked up what I could from him and added it to my own trading strategy toolkit. If you're willing to set aside your ego and have an open mind, you can pick up a wide range of effective tactics from other people. You never know when they might come in handy.

TRADING IS YOUR BUSINESS

When I lost half of my account on a few bad trades, I didn't want to take responsibility for my loss. I was embarrassed, and I didn't want anyone to find out what I'd done. After stewing about the loss for a while, I made the choice to learn more about trading so I could revamp my techniques. In order to do that, I had to admit that my losses were my own fault because I hadn't taken enough time to seek out mentors. I'd been overly confident about my own abilities. Admitting that weakness helped me make the right decisions to get my account back to even.

It's easy to look back and see what you should have done and could have done to avoid some of the low points. Timing is such a key part of success in stock trading, and with the market changing every second, it's incredibly difficult to get it right. The should-have-could-have mentality can take hold so easily, even when you do well. If you make a good trade and capture $1,000, only to see the stock go up a little more afterward, it's tempting to think, "I should have held onto it a little longer. Then I would have made $1,500 instead." That kind of mentality is a trap, and it can cause you to doubt and second-guess everything. It can also rob you of the joy of every win.

Appreciate every win, no matter how small, without obsessing over how you might have gotten even more money out of the deal. Instead, look at it as a business deal where you made a real profit. The danger of obsessing over small wins that should have been bigger is that you'll start making rash decisions. Instead, stick to your business plan and watch the small wins pile up.

When I encourage you not to make emotional decisions, I'm not suggesting you have to become like a robot. We're all human, and you're going to react emotionally to both wins and losses. However, in the end, you have to look at your overall experience in a positive way. You can only do that if you handle the low points correctly. When you take a loss, first ask yourself if you followed your plan. If you did follow your plan and still took a loss, then determine how you can learn from the loss to make your next trade better.

Likewise, when you make a good trade, be happy with how you executed it and ask yourself what you can do to make the next trade just as good or better. I feel both happy and frustrated every single day I'm trading. You can't take emotion out of it completely. However, I try not to let my feelings determine the next trade I make. Whatever happens, I take a positive spin on it, move on quickly, and let things go, whether it's a win or a loss.

BE QUIET AND FOCUSED

People watch movies about Wall Street and only see the business from the broker's point of view. Even then, the story always exaggerates the reality. They show you the wild parties with cocaine all over the tables and prostitutes wandering from room to room, and they show brokers making huge wins, pulling in hundreds of thousands of dollars on individual trades. That's not how it works, especially if you want to use trading as a tool to get out of debt. These movies depict a lifestyle that has very little resemblance to real life, so if that's what you're looking for, I would strongly encourage you to look somewhere else.

What does the world of stock trading actually look like? Let's consider a company called Citadel. Back in the day, if you had walked into a trading office, you would have seen a huge community of traders, all talking and making a bunch of noise as they placed trades over the phone. Today, when you walk into Citadel, you see a room full of computers and very few people. A handful of employees monitor the computers, but the computers make all of the trades. Citadel is one of the most profitable trading firms. They've only had one losing month in ten years, but it's so quiet inside their building that a casual observer would have no idea that anything of significance was taking place.

When you see the Hollywood depiction of trading stocks, where people experience extreme high and lows—making $100,000 then losing $100,000 back-to-back—just remember, that's not what you want. You want a trading strategy that is more even-keeled. Ideally, your trading day should consist of you sitting at a desk, maybe listening to stock news, and quietly making trades on your computer—an environment not unlike Citadel. When you're trading, you should be as focused as if you were writing a book. The last thing you need is a loud, obnoxious environment.

In fact, in my experience, many successful traders have personalities quite unlike the stereotype that is so common in movies. Hollywood traders have big emotions, and they're always shouting and running around. In reality, to succeed at trading, it's best to maintain focus and discipline, almost like a monk.

YOUR NICHE

Once you embrace the idea that trading is a business rather than a form of gambling, you'll realize that the market is very expansive. There are numerous strategies you can utilize and countless industries to invest in. If you want to win the competition and become profitable, you need to find your niche in the market, a place where you have an edge.

When I started, I was drawn to biotech stocks because I had a biology degree. I figured if I focused on that specific sector, my knowledge of the industry would give me an advantage over other investors. In any other sector, I wouldn't know the news or the companies. This kind of niche strategy, focusing on one industry or technique, is a smart way to build your success. In the next chapter, we'll take a closer look at how you can identify your niche.

CHAPTER FIVE

Focusing on a Niche

To discover my niche, I used a combination of my personality and my interests. In terms of personality, I learned very quickly that I prefer fast-moving trades. The life of a day trader appealed to me because I craved instant gratification and fast results. At the same time, I wanted my profit to remain fairly steady over a long period of time. Although day trading offered the excitement of instant results, it didn't fit my timeframe. Since I had a full-time job, I couldn't sit in front of my computer all day looking at stocks, so somehow, I needed a strategy that fit my need for consistency while also meeting my desire for faster moving stocks.

TRADING STRATEGIES

There are several different types of trading styles to choose from. By understanding how they work, you can find the one that works best for you.

SCALP TRADING

Scalp trading specializes in taking profits on small price changes. It tends to be ultra-fast, because you're in and out of a position within a minute. Typically, you make these trades based on some big news event that has just broken or another catalyst in the market, but you have to make quick decisions. It's a high-risk/high-reward strategy that requires a lot of skill.

DAY TRADING

Generally speaking, day trading means you open and close your position during the day. For example, you might buy into a stock in the morning then close it that same afternoon. This kind of trading can be highly profitable, but it's difficult and involves a lot of risk.

SWING TRADING

In swing trading, you hold onto a stock for one to three days. My mentor Jason Bond does a lot of swing trading. It requires analyzing a lot of technical information and studying multiple charts. You can get good returns from this style of trading, but you have to be good at timing. That means you have to recognize entry points, and you have to possess good chart analysis skills.

CATALYST TRADING

Catalyst trading has worked well for me, particularly in the early stages of my trading career. Basically, catalyst trading involves looking for upcoming events that will cause a stock to move. For catalyst trading in the biotech space, I look for potentially significant events two to four weeks in the future and buy accordingly. The specific catalyst might be an earnings call, or it might be some data that is scheduled to become public—anything that might potentially move the stock. Success in this kind of trading requires being able to recognize an upcoming catalyst and use chart analysis to time a point of entry.

INVESTING

When people talk about investing in a stock, as opposed to trading in a stock, in simplest terms, they are referring to buying and holding a stock over a very long period of time. Rather than a day or a few weeks, the timeline might be years.

IDENTIFY YOUR TRADING ADVANTAGES

There are other forms of stock trading, but the short list outlined above covers the most common investing styles. As you go down the list, you'll notice that the time commitment gets longer. Scalp trading is literally a second-by-second activity, while investing takes years. To determine which one is right for you, take inventory of your own needs, preferences, and goals. If you want more stability and have long-term goals, then you should probably choose an investing style of trading rather than the instant gratification and risks of scalp trading. From my experience with clients, most people do best with catalyst trading, because it provides the stability and fundamentals analysis that people like along with the excitement of faster movement like swing trading.

When I finally developed my trading style, I focused on catalyst trading. It works well for someone with a full-time job. I could do my fundamental research at night, place trades in the morning, and do some light monitoring throughout the day. I knew that if I could achieve success with catalyst trading, I could build up my account enough to adopt some of the faster-moving trading styles later on.

On the other hand, for people who have little knowledge of stocks but still want to play the market, a long-term investment style works best. The benefit of investing is that you don't need to put much time into it. The downside is that your returns aren't very high, unless you're as skillful and smart in your investments as Warren Buffett. With long-term investing, based on my experience, you can expect between 8 to 10 percent returns. If you want bigger returns than that, you'll have to sacrifice a bit of stability for something faster and riskier where gains compound a lot quicker.

I figured if I could master catalyst trading, then I could try swing trading, and if I mastered swing trading, then I could try day trading and scalp trading. That was my plan, and that's exactly what I did. What helped me succeed at every style was picking an industry that interested me. By picking a specific market that you're knowledgeable about, you narrow down your options. That makes decision-making easier when you're starting out.

I don't know a ton about the medical side of biotech, but my interest in that sector helped me learn and develop an edge over the average person. I'm not a doctor, so I can't analyze clinical trial results. However, I have gained an above-average level of expertise about the industry, and that's all you need to do.

I have focused on and followed biotech for a long time. It's similar to being a Los Angeles Lakers fan. If you're a fan of the team, you get to know the players, follow all the trades, and have a thorough understanding of how the team is doing. That's how it is when you pick a specific industry sector to focus on. The longer you stick with it, the more you learn about it, and the greater your advantage becomes.

To clarify, I believe specific sector knowledge is far less important than your personality and timeframe when it comes to selecting a trading style, but it can help you get started by narrowing your focus. Many people I talk to don't recognize their specific industry advantage. If that's your situation, then consider your career background and experience. For example, someone who has worked in the oil industry has a huge advantage when it comes to investing in oil stocks because of their personal knowledge of the industry. Think carefully about the knowledge, experience, or skills you possess that give you an edge over the average trader in a specific sector, and you'll start out ahead of the curve.

PICK YOUR TIMEFRAME

Many people who get into trading have full-time jobs and families. Whatever your situation, it's important to pick a strategy that fits with your schedule and won't interfere with other obligations. If you're a day trader or scalp trader, you have to sit in front of your computer all day long, carefully watching the markets. If you're retired or have a really lax job, this might work for you. Otherwise, you will struggle to make it work. I actually did a little bit of scalp trading early on by getting into work incredibly early. Since the markets opened at 6:30 a.m. Pacific time, I had a few hours to make some scalp trades before my real job began. That's not possible for many people.

For swing trading, the hold period is one to three days, so you don't necessarily have to sit in front of your computer all the time, but you still have to play an active role. That means staying in tune with the markets. Many swing traders check stock prices on their phones and set alerts. This might still be a problem in certain jobs.

When I worked in real estate, catalyst trading fit best with my schedule, which is another reason I recommend it to so many new traders. I held onto stocks for one to four weeks so I didn't have to watch every single tick on the stock prices. I still had to analyze charts and fundamentals, but it didn't consume much time compared to other strategies. I could work at my desk or go into a meeting without worrying about my positions because I had a combination of factors working in my favor.

Long-term investing occurs over a year or more, so it doesn't take up much time from day to day. You still need to do your research to make sure you invest wisely, especially if you want to get above the average 8 to 10 percent return. In fact, I would say that fundamental research is more important with investing, but once you've selected your stock, you don't have to monitor it very often.

Contrast this with scalp trading, where there's almost no research at all. A decision is made in a few seconds based on a near-term chart pattern or some news item. Day trades are similar. The longer the timeframe, the more research you must do on the front end and the less monitoring of your position you have to do afterward. Ultimately, short-term trading is heavily affected by the current market state and the news, which means it changes rapidly all the time, and you have to stay on top of it.

Catalyst trading falls in the middle. For example, in my situation, I had to do a bit of research up front, looking at upcoming drug release dates, industry conferences, or company conference calls. I also researched each company's past successes and failures with their drugs. Many biotech companies are too new to produce earnings, so I didn't have to do much earnings analysis, unless their drug had already gone to market. In those instances, I looked at the trajectory of their sales.

You have multiple options, so pick a trading style that works for your timeframe, your personality, and your personal knowledge. Make it work for you, and your chances of success will be much greater.

TRIAL AND ERROR

Many beginners feel drawn to day trading because of the huge potential rewards it offers, but since they don't yet understand why stocks move up or down, they struggle to get those big returns. With catalyst trading, you pick your niche and then identify the catalysts that might cause a stock in your niche to go up or down. It's a nice combination of fundamental research and technical analysis that can lead to higher-percentage returns in all of your trades.

Some trial and error is always required; it's part of everyone's journey. Even today, when I implement a new strategy, I often make errors while trying to perfect it. By asking yourself a few key questions, you can determine if the niche and strategy you picked are right for you.

First, ask yourself if your risk tolerance is high, medium, or low. Generally speaking, the longer-term strategies are less risky. Second, ask yourself how much time you want to spend each day watching trades. If you have a little bit of free time, catalyst trading might be perfect for you. On the other hand, if you prefer to buy a stock and not look at it for three years, you need to focus on an investment strategy. Finally, ask yourself if you like to act quickly and reactively or prefer to do a lot of research and planning beforehand. Again, the long-term strategies require more research up front and less reactive decision-making along the way.

Personally, I prefer the quick and reactive style rather than doing a lot of fundamental aftermarket research, but that's just my personality. What is your personality? Choose your approach accordingly, and you can't go wrong.

LEARN FROM MENTORS

Looking for a good mentor can be overwhelming. There are countless books you can buy, podcasts you can listen to, and websites you can visit. How do you choose the right mentor for you? First, define the strategy that makes sense for your desired timeframe and personality. That information will allow you to seek out the best mentor, financial podcast, or book to help you learn and grow.

On my journey, I reached out to Jason Bond and joined his website because he had a lot of information about chart pattern analysis. At the time, I was focused primarily on catalysts and fundamentals, so adding chart pattern and technical analysis to my toolkit seemed like a good idea. Out of all the possible mentors, he offered the specific information I needed to improve my specific strategy.

At Raging Bull, the online trading community, I also met another mentor in Petra Hess. She does a lot of pattern work and focuses on various mathematical indicators that can affect entry and exit times, such as simple moving averages, exponential moving averages, and money flow index. I saw value in her expertise, so I made a point to learn from her techniques as well.

Over the years, it has helped me tremendously to listen to and learn from the various trading styles of other successful people. Thanks to a wide range of mentors, I can readily adopt a wide array of trading strategies and techniques to maximize my success. I can't emphasize the need for mentors strongly enough. Look for people who can best speak to your needs and help you grow.

HOW TO GROW FROM YOUR NICHE

Once you find a niche, you can become an expert in your chosen industry. That's a much easier task if you select an industry that you've worked in because then you start with a leg up. If you pick an industry that's brand new to you, you start from square one. You can certainly go that route, but if you do that, I recommend narrowing your focus to a single sector within that industry. That makes it easier to learn about relevant companies and to gain understanding about which news items might impact your sector. That can give you a competitive edge over someone in your industry who has a broader scope. If you're into hedge funds, for example, you have many people who are richer and smarter competing against you, but you can beat them if you have a small niche to grow your portfolio.

Once you master your niche, you can branch off into other sectors, just as you can branch off into other trading styles. Though I began with biotech stocks, and I still invest in them, I eventually moved into other sectors, such as gold and tech stocks. When you feel like you're ready to try new things, work some trial and error into your plan. See if you can figure out what else works for you. Before you know it, you'll have ten to fifteen different profit buckets you can utilize for different market conditions.

With multiple strategies in play, you can see which one is giving you better returns and put more focus into it. This approach ensures that you have different avenues to make money and grow your trading business, regardless of market conditions.

CHAPTER SIX

Baby Steps to Big Results

Real, lasting success in the stock market began when I developed an effective business plan and stuck to it. My business plan involved following upcoming catalysts in the biotech sector, which proved to be a reliable niche. Because I had some experience in the sector, I was able to predict with a fair degree of accuracy what was going to happen in the market each week, month, or year. Since the biotech industry is constantly developing and testing new products, there tends to be a steady stream of catalysts.

When I first started discovering these catalysts, I realized that buying and holding stocks through these specific event dates had a lot in common with gambling. If I accurately predicted positive data, I could make a lot of money, but if I got it wrong, I would lose a lot. Although this worked in my favor more often than not, I figured there had to be a better way, so I developed a better business plan.

RUN-UP TRADING

For my new strategy, I began capitalizing on what I like to call the run-up to the event, rather than holding a stock through the actual data release. I bought into a stock four to six weeks ahead of a data event, held onto it for three to four weeks, then sold it just before a catalyst occurred. In many cases, anticipation in the market would cause the value of the stock to rise prior to the catalyst. Although this technique didn't allow me to capture big 100 to 300 percent moves, it reliably yielded an average of 30 percent wins almost every time. On a good catalyst play, I could get as much as 40 to 50 percent—occasionally even 100 percent—returns before a data event occurred.

This strategy helped me to gain confidence in my predictive abilities. Instead of watching my account swing back and forth between huge losses and gains, I grew my account consistently through small, compounding successes. This technique helped me grind my account back to even after I lost half my account, and once I did that, I regained the confidence I'd lost through my early mistakes. My mistakes at least taught me what not to do, so I avoided the kinds of risky trades I'd made in the beginning and focused on small wins. When those small wins started rolling in, I began to achieve real, lasting success for the first time.

BABY STEPS FOR INCREMENTAL SUCCESS

Don't be in a hurry. Take baby steps. In the beginning, for a while, give all your focus to your niche and your initial game plan, and don't let fear or greed start influencing your actions. When I'm making a run-up trade, greed wants me to keep holding that stock through the upcoming data event in the hope of a much bigger gain. I have to deny that greed and keep pursuing those incremental gains. Greed will tell you to swing for the fences every single time you're at bat, instead of going for consistent singles and doubles.

It's the same reason I got into options early on. Greed made me reach for those huge returns, even if I had to risk big losses in the process. When you swing for the back fence, it might occasionally work out for you, but if you want to develop and grow your portfolio over a long period of time, you have to rely on a repeatable strategy. Otherwise, you end up putting your money all over the place in the market, hoping for the best. Pulling the arm of the slot machine isn't a defined strategy. You can't depend on hope, so create a consistent strategy and make careful, intentional decisions.

I meet people all the time who want to become full-time traders because they think it offers a great job with a ton of freedom. The truth is, you don't get the freedom right out of the gate. You can't simply dive in and expect to immediately reap the rewards. I spoke to one individual who was making $200,000 a year at his job and wanted to quit and immediately start day trading full time. It is extremely foolish to throw away a $200,000 a year job when you're going to start at zero in an industry where you might actually lose money in the beginning.

Gamblers don't like to take baby steps. They prefer a few big wins over many small wins, but that approach loses people a lot of money. The beginning trader might say, "I used to make $200,000 a year at my old job, so now I need to make $200,000 trading," so they feel compelled to make a bunch of high-risk trades.

When I hear people talking this way, I always warn them. "Before you quit your job, consider your track record with the stock market. Have you ever traded before? Have you proven to yourself that you have a strategy for consistently making money in the market?"

By the time I left my real estate job, I had already made quite a bit of money in the stock market. Losing my regular income wasn't a problem. In fact, I could have quit sooner. However, if I'd quit during the first year, I might have been in trouble. I wasn't making enough consistent income in stocks during my first year in real estate, so it would have created an unnecessary risk. I had to wait until I had the right strategy in place, with small wins coming in consistently.

If you leave your full-time job too early and then hit a low point in your stock trading, it might prove catastrophic. People tend to do it for emotional, rather than logical, reasons. "I'm going for it! I'm leaving everything behind, and I'm going to hit it big on the stock market!"

That kind of thinking is a danger you must always be aware of. It applies to every single trade you make. When you put too much emotional stake into your trades, you're far more likely to sell too early, buy too late, or make other reactionary mistakes. When you lose a bunch of money doing this, it will damage your confidence and might set you back. Many people never recover.

START SMALL, LOSE SMALL

Instead of putting all of your money in the stock market right out of the gate, start with an amount you can afford to lose without seriously affecting your net worth. If you have $25,000 in savings, don't throw it all into the market and cross your fingers. Instead, consider starting with

$1,500. That's your test money. You can afford to lose it all in the process of learning different trading strategies. The amount you choose to start with should be small enough that it won't negatively impact your lifestyle if you lose it all. You could start as small as $100. It's up to you.

Ultimately, you have to be willing and able to lose all of the money you start with. If you do end up losing it, consider it a rite of passage, like paying tuition to get your college degree. All of that money you paid for college classes wound up earning you a degree that could get you a good-paying job. In the same way, you might lose that $1,500 in the market, but you'll learn lessons that will contribute to long-term success later on.

When you have the mentality that you'll almost certainly lose your starting money, it helps to keep your early trading positions small. It counters the greed that sometimes causes reckless behavior. I didn't start with much, so I didn't have the opportunity to lose a fortune right out of the gate. However, I've seen people get started with $200,000 or $300,000 and lose half of it almost immediately. From a psychological standpoint, that kind of early loss is hard to bounce back from.

PAPER TRADING

If you want to practice buying and selling securities without using real money, you can start with paper trading. Various online platforms allow you to place paper trades, which are simulated trades. This is a good way to practice and learn the market so you know what to expect when you shift to real money. It eliminates any risk, though it also eliminates the reward. However, it's a safe way to test out various strategies.

Personally, I think it's better to have a little skin in the game. If you're paper trading and you hit a big return, you'll regret it. "If I had been trading for real, I would have made a fortune!" That's a frustrating place to be. In fact, when I tried paper trading, I found that I didn't learn enough to make the process worthwhile. Since no real money was at stake, I often failed to keep track of what I was doing.

When you open a real account with a broker and have positions in real stocks, you have the motivation to track them. Since you have money involved, the stakes are higher, even if you start with very small positions. You might not make any significant money on your small positions—and you have to pay your broker and commission fees—but you'll learn faster and get a better sense of what it feels like to trade.

A BUSINESS PLAN FOR EVERY POSITION

My first baby step was opening a brokerage account on

TradeKing with $1,500. A friend of mine told me they had the cheapest commissions at the time: five dollars a trade. Nowadays, broker commissions have gotten much cheaper, so you can find fees as low as three dollars per trade.

After my early missteps, when I realized I had no idea what I was doing, I decided to create a detailed plan. I bought a large binder and a sheaf of blank paper. Then I sat down and created a business plan for each catalyst I saw ahead of individual stocks. I created a chart so I could write the prices I wanted to buy and sell at.

When you buy a stock, every day you have to ask yourself, "Should I sell this now, or should I hold?" By having a plan that tracks your optimal course of action, you can answer this question easily. Look at the plan and see how the value of the stock aligns with your projections for that day.

After I had some experience under my belt, I didn't need the binder because the planning process became second nature to me. I do offer a watch list for my subscribers, however, that tracks numerous stock prices. This process helps my subscribers stay connected to their business plans with each stock. I use the watch list myself sometimes. It's a great tool that would have benefited me tremendously in the beginning.

BABY STEPS INTO NEW STRATEGIES

Every time I develop a new trading strategy, I start off slowly. I eased into catalyst trading, and once I'd mastered it, I eased into other trading styles to build a larger account. After a few years of that, I started participating in day trading, scalp trading, swing trading, and investing. I even do a bit of options trading now. With a portfolio as big as mine, I can't afford to have all of my capital tied up in one strategy. Anything that makes money is now fair game, but in the beginning, my efforts were very focused. When you're just getting started, maintain that narrow focus. Don't worry about learning every trading style. You'll have plenty of time for that later. Ease into everything.

To reach the point I'm at now, where I regularly use multiple strategies, I had to take baby steps for each technique. After mastering catalyst trading, I didn't say, "Since my account is bigger now, I'll use the whole thing for day trading and maybe catch a huge windfall." Instead, I tested the waters in day trading, just as if I were starting all over again. I had to discover if day trading worked for my personality and timeframe, if I was any good at it, and if I understood how much work to put into it. That's what you have to do with every new trading style you adopt.

This is why I say you have to be willing to lose some money in the beginning. You're learning, testing, and figuring out what works for you. Once you learn what works for you, which techniques you're best at, then you'll start making a consistent profit. I got to the point I'm at today by slowly building my portfolio and gradually trying new things.

Along the way, I've learned that taking big leaps isn't ever really necessary. I made over $1 million in trading this year, and I got to this point by taking baby steps all along the way. When people learn how much I'm making at trading, they often assume I've gotten there though huge trades. They assume the $1 million this year must have come from a single $800,000 trade, but that's not the way I operate. I am grinding out that money every day. Occasionally, I have a big win, but what makes the difference in the long run is stacking up smaller wins all day long using different strategies. Every day, I pursue the small wins, and it works. I don't need to chase the big, risky positions, and I discourage others from doing it.

THE NERVES WILL DISAPPEAR...EVENTUALLY

You don't necessarily need to embrace a wide range of trading strategies. As your account starts to grow, you can simply increase the number of shares in your positions using the exact same strategy. For example, if you would have bought 1,000 shares of a stock in the beginning, maybe you increase it to 2,000 or 3,000 when your account gets bigger. You might be allotting the same percentage of your account to the position so that it grows naturally as your account grows. When I first started, I often bought only fifty shares of individual stocks. These days, I sometimes buy 20,000 shares. I'm not acting more reckless now than I was in the beginning. I simply have more to work with because of what I've learned over time.

From an emotional standpoint, every time I put in a trade in those early days, even with positions as small as fifty shares, my heart nearly beat out of my chest. Eventually, as my confidence grew, I didn't feel quite so nervous the second I put in a trade, but when I moved into day trading, the anxiety started all over again. Sometimes, I felt so nervous I could hardly contain myself. Of course, now that I've mastered a wide range of trading styles, each individual trade is nothing to me. I am much calmer and more comfortable with the process, and I spend my days chatting with people and monitoring news events. I don't get the rush of fear I used to. If that fear does creep in, it's because I'm doing something reckless, like putting too much money into a single position. That's usually a sign that I'm making a mistake and need to reconsider my approach.

Believe it or not, in terms of anxiety, full-time stock trading feels a lot like my time as an EMT. After a while, an EMT has seen so many vehicle accidents, heart attack victims, and tragedies that they don't feel nervous on the way to the scene anymore. It no longer fazes them to see people in horrible conditions. The same thing happens with doctors. An ER doctor can perform surgery in life-or-death situations without being mentally or emotionally affected by it. They've just seen it all so many times. With stock trading, the initial anxiety wears off with experience. As your self-doubt and fear diminish, you'll make trades more confidently, and your portfolio will grow.

COMPOUNDING SMALL WINS

Even if you don't hit gigantic winners, by taking baby steps, you will consistently achieve smaller wins for sustainable growth. In the beginning, it might seem impossible to get enough small wins to make a big difference, but I'm here to tell you, it's not only possible but likely. As long as you take baby steps, start small, and make a business plan for each trade, your personal gains will add up over time, and before you know it, you'll see truly impressive results. I can tell you from experience, that's the path to long-term success. Personally, I'd much rather get a whole bunch of small wins rather than the occasional big winner.

PART THREE

The Personal Gains from Trading Success

CHAPTER SEVEN

Time Investment for Growth

It took me a while to see any real trading growth in my portfolio. For a long time, it felt like I was stuck in neutral, but once my account started growing, the money accumulated quickly. That's the thing with exponential growth: it starts slow, but when it ramps up, it becomes breathtaking.

THE LEAP OF FAITH PAYS OFF

As I mentioned earlier, I lost half of my account during my first year of trading, and then I spent a long time trying to get it all back. It felt like a long, hard slog. It wasn't until I made more money in the stock market in one year than I did at my real estate job that I realized I might be able to make trading work for me.

That year, I made roughly $30,000 at my job and a little over $40,000 at trading. That was the first time I truly believed stock trading could become a full-time job, though I was nervous about giving up the security of a consistent paycheck. By 2015, I was making $500,000 a year at trading, but I still held on to the real estate job. Looking back, I should have quit sooner. As soon as I could consistently make the same income at trading as I did in real estate, I should have made the transition.

I didn't get serious about quitting real estate until October of 2015. That was the fateful moment when I had that annual review with my boss in which he said, "You're doing a good job. We want to give you a raise, but you have to put more effort and more passion into this." That comment helped me to see what I had been unwilling to see on my own. I still wanted to keep my guaranteed salary, but I knew at that point that I couldn't do it. I had to follow my passion, and I'd laid down a solid enough foundation to do it.

Still, quitting real estate required a leap of faith. I don't know why I held on for so long. I had this irrational fear that said, "What if the day you quit is the last day you ever make money from stock trading? What if the market turns bad right after you leave real estate and you can no longer achieve the same success you had before you quit?" In retrospect, these are silly, irrational thoughts, but they ran through my head constantly until I finally took that leap.

As soon as I quit, I went out and bought a plastic table and put it in the living room of my apartment. Then I placed a couple of computer screens on it, and that was my workstation. I sat down that first morning and began trading full time, and I've never looked back.

By increasing the amount of time I dedicated to trading, I learned more than I ever had before. Rather than losing money the day I quit my job, I started making a lot more. I no longer had to worry about commuting to work or dividing my attention between competing job responsibilities. As a result, I was able to multiply and scale my profits much faster, and my earning curve became exponential.

I treated stock trading like a real job. In other words, I gave it my full attention throughout the workday, even though I no longer had a boss looking over my shoulder. Some people struggle to work hard when they don't have any immediate supervision. Too much freedom is bad for people who lack motivation and a strong work ethic. Once you leave your regular job to start trading full time, you're going to have to self-motivate constantly. You'll have to make yourself get up in the morning and sit down at that computer. Nobody's going to tell you to stop playing video games or browsing meaningless websites. Nobody's going to yell at you for taking a long break in the middle of the day for no reason. You have to become your own boss and practice self-control.

I treated stock trading like a regular job and made myself work full eight-hour days. With that time commitment, I was able to invest more often, and I wound up with six times the returns that I had while working at the real estate firm. Simply by concentrating completely on trading, I took my strategy to the next level.

Your initial growth will be slow, but once you reach a point where you can give trading your full attention, then it's time to take that leap. After that, you'll start to see this same kind of exponential growth, but only if you make the commitment. If you're not there yet, be patient. Keep taking those baby steps. The big leap will happen before you know it.

TIME IS THE DIFFERENCE

Any aspect of trading that you want to master simply takes time. The more time you put into it, the more you'll get out of it, but trading doesn't need to be a sprint. If anything, it's more like a marathon, so maintain a steady pace.

Take note of where you are right now. Are you brand new to the stock market, or do you have some experience? If you've never made a trade before, you're at a very different starting point than someone who is already making $40,000 a year in the market and thinking about quitting their full-time job. Strategize accordingly. Don't get ahead of yourself. The big returns will come in time.

Regardless of your starting point, the key to making this work is to keep learning about stock trading each and every day. Even if you still have another full-time job, use your free time for trading. Those extra hours will pay off in time. If you're brand new to trading, that extra time will get you to a point where you can make trading your full-time job much faster. It's worth losing out on a little leisure time during the early stages. Trust me—you won't regret it.

EXPONENTIAL GROWTH

When I say I began to experience exponential growth, what do I mean? What did that look like? The first year I felt like I truly succeeded, I made $40,000 in the stock market. That was also, as I said, the year I started making more at trading than I did at my regular job. I quit real estate the next year, when I made $500,000 in stock trading. The year after that, 2016, I made $1.1 million, and in 2017, I made over $1.2 million.

The growth has been encouraging. I expect to eventually hit a ceiling, but that ceiling is clearly much higher in stock trading than in most other careers. Don't forget, I started my stock trading at less than zero, thanks to my massive student loan debt.

Of course, even though I make over a million dollars a

year now, I don't trade with that much money. On the contrary, I usually trade with about $250,000, and I take out money to pay myself twice a month, just as if it were a regular paycheck. Paying myself twice a month helps me to look at trading as a real job with a steady income. In that way, it's like my real estate analyst job, but it's a lot more fun and has a lot more potential for income growth.

WHAT TRADING CAN GIVE YOU

Quitting my previous job gave me the extra time I needed to expand everything I was doing in relation to trading. I became more focused in learning different strategies and styles, and I developed a better plan. That's what enabled me to try different trading strategies and delve into other industries in the market. I also had the time to seek out more mentors through books and podcasts.

Every single new opportunity provided by my newfound free time contributed to the growth of my profits. Besides the financial benefit, however, devoting myself full-time to trading also improved my personal life because I no longer had to navigate competing job responsibilities. I could finally embrace my real passion fully.

Though I've said I was fortunate to live on the West Coast, where the market opened at 6:30 a.m.—early enough that I could make some trades before my real job began—it might have actually hindered my progress. Having those morning hours to trade might have encouraged me to hold on to the real estate job longer than I needed to. Whatever your situation, if you want to achieve consistent success in trading, you have to give it as much time as you reasonably can. Don't quit your job rashly, of course. Wait until you can afford to make the move, but when the time is right, take that leap. In the meantime, give your free time to learning and strategizing.

CHAPTER EIGHT

Freedom of Choice

Traveling the world never seemed to be an option for my family. First of all, we simply didn't have enough money to take long trips. Second, both of my parents worked full time, so they struggled to find the time to travel. When you work for someone else, you can't just decide to head out of town whenever you want. You might get two weeks of vacation time a year, so your timeframe is limited. Although I often dreamed of a life of freedom in which I would have the money and time to travel whenever I wanted, I never thought it was something I would get to experience.

Of course, my family did enjoy an occasional vacation. In fact, we had a few memorable trips as a family, going to places like Alaska and Hawaii, but they were few and far between. I'm not suggesting that I had a difficult childhood or that I was deprived. On the contrary, I think my family experience was fairly typical of an average middle-class family. However, now that I'm a trader, I enjoy a freedom that I never imagined. As long as I have a computer and an internet connection, I can work from practically anywhere, and I've been successful enough that I can afford to take extended vacations any time I feel like it. Stock trading has given me that freedom.

This has been tremendously beneficial in my personal life. A couple of years ago, my girlfriend enrolled in optometry school. We were living in LA at the time, but the school was located all the way in Tennessee. If I'd had a normal job, this would have created a real problem for our relationship. Fortunately, because I'm a full-time stock trader, I was able to pack up and follow her to Tennessee with no inconvenience and no damage to my career. We were able to start a new life together in a completely new location, and I never missed a day of work. I can't imagine another type of job that provides such freedom.

You can live practically anywhere in the world and still trade in the stock market. As long as you're willing to put in the work, you can make this career succeed in LA, New York, Tennessee, or a tropical island in the middle of the Pacific Ocean (as long as that tropical island has internet access). I know quite a few successful traders who routinely travel from city to city, even country to country, seeing the world while they work. They never stay in one place long. I don't personally enjoy that kind of digital nomad lifestyle. It doesn't fit the way I want to live, but many successful people in the world of stock trading love it. You might be one of those people. Does the thought of moving from place to place, visiting cities all over the world whenever you feel like it, appeal to you? You can have that lifestyle.

THE FREEDOM TO TRAVEL

Although some of these world travelers will occasionally take multiple days off from work during their travels, I don't enjoy missing days of trading. I always think about the money I might have made during those missed days. I like the fact that I can take a vacation and still get some work done at the same time. Two years ago, I spent a week and a half in Hawaii. Last summer, I went with my parents and my brother to Norway, the land of our ancestors. When my girlfriend finished her master's program in New Hampshire, I was able to travel to her graduation on short notice.

I could travel a lot more than I do, but I also have the freedom to choose not to travel. My life as a stock trader provides me with incredible flexibility, so I can live the way I want to live. I never would have come close to this much personal freedom if I'd continued to work as a real estate analyst.

THE FREEDOM TO EXPERIENCE NEW THINGS

As you grow your trading business, your success will open up many new opportunities for you, increasing your freedom in almost every area of life. In my opinion, time is the most valuable thing we have, so being able to take a day off whenever I want is a big deal. If the market is dead in the middle of the day, I can say, "Nothing's happening today. I think I'll just take the rest of the day off." If you suddenly decide you want to spend the afternoon hiking or going to see some friends or taking in an early movie, you can do that. You can do exactly what you want at almost any time of the day.

Also, if you work hard and achieve financial success through trading, you can treat yourself to luxury items you've always wanted but could never afford. What are the ways you would treat yourself if you had complete financial freedom? Maybe there's a certain kind of car you've always wanted to own. Maybe you'd love to own a big, spacious house with an indoor swimming pool. Maybe you'd enjoy a closet full of nice clothes. Or perhaps you have some specific hobby that demands a lot of money.

For me, treating myself meant enjoying fine dining and good food. In my old job, I often agonized about whether or not I could afford to eat out at a nice restaurant without stretching my budget too far. Now, with my success, I can enjoy a nice steak at a fine steakhouse without having to worry about it. I could eat an expensive steak every night of the week, if I wanted to. I also greatly appreciate the ability to spend plenty of time with friends and family. I never have to choose between work and loved ones.

Which aspect of this freedom will you enjoy most? It's different for each person, but regardless of what you value, the life of a successful stock trader empowers you to pursue your favorite things.

FREEDOM FROM DEBT

The most significant freedom I have experienced as a stock trader is becoming debt-free. I don't owe money to anyone. I don't have to worry about how much of my paycheck will go to pay student loans, a mortgage, a car payment, or credit card bills. I made enough to pay off all of my debts.

I've always despised debt. I hate that constant anxiety you feel when you owe someone money, so I've made it a point to avoid it. All of the money I make in trading is mine. I earned it, and I get to keep it.

When I had massive student loan debt, it always lingered in the back of my mind as a constant source of tension and stress. How am I going to pay this off? When am I going to pay this off? That's why I started working the day after I graduated college. I wanted to pay off that debt as quickly as possible.

When you owe a large amount of money, whether that's student loan debt, a mortgage, a car payment, or medical bills, you worry constantly about losing your job. If you get laid off, you might lose your car, your house, or other assets. You might get sued. Those kinds of scenarios always scared me.

I've met many people in the last few years who feel the same way. They live with constant anxiety because they're paying for a house, cars, insurance, medical bills, their kids' school, and a whole host of other things. The constant anxiety caused by debt steals your joy and makes it harder to enjoy your life. You can't even appreciate the good things as much as you should because of what might happen.

What if I have a medical emergency and suddenly my family is crushed under a mountain of medical bills? What will happen to my family if I get fired? What if I miss a month on my credit card bills?

These are all common fears. It's bad enough when you live alone, but when you have a family to take care of, those fears are compounded. *What if my family gets thrown out onto the street? What if all of my mounting debt damages my children's futures?* That's no way to live, which is why I wanted to dig my way out of debt as quickly as possible. Now that I'm successful and my big debts are all paid off, I try to avoid acquiring new debt as much as possible. It feels wonderful not to owe anyone anything.

That desire to live debt free was always with me, but I never would have gotten there without the success of stock trading. It's about more than avoiding debt, however. I want to be free to use my own money as I please. From a psychological standpoint, it feels much better. Once I paid off my student loans, I was able to start creating a financial safety net through a savings account. With that safety net in place, I now use my money for whatever I want. I feel healthier and happier, and my day-to-day life is vastly better than it was before. Part of the reason I mentor other people is because I want them to experience this better life. I see people struggling, I hear their stories, and I want them to enjoy this level of freedom.

BUYING WITHOUT GUILT

Once you dig your way out of debt, you no longer have to worry about paying anyone else. At that point, you can begin building a nest egg for yourself and saving money for the big things in life that you've always wanted. Create a rainy-day fund just in case something goes wrong, such as a medical emergency or a loved one in need. After that, you can kick back and relax, because you have a safety net in place that will enable you to survive the hard times.

You can also buy nice things without feeling guilty. You're never eating into your budget or draining away money that you need to pay off debt. You can enjoy a nice meal or buy a new phone without feeling bad about it. You never have to say, "I shouldn't have bought this nice, new thing. I should have used the money to pay my credit card bill."

I don't believe that this level of success is only accessible to a select few. By using the mindset, tactics, and techniques for trading that I've laid out in this book, you, too, can earn the freedom to enjoy your life instead of living in the shadow of debt. Take ownership over your money and buy what you want without guilt.

CHAPTER NINE

Successes Shared

The most immediate reward of successful stock trading has been the money I've made, of course. However, on top of the money, I've been able to help many other people change their perspective on their past failures and future successes, and that's an incredible feeling. By sharing the knowledge I've acquired, I get to show people a path to a better and happier life.

Every day, I receive emails from people who tell me they are hesitant to try stock trading again because of mistakes they've made in the past. They want to rebuild their accounts, but they lack confidence in their ability to do so. Others have quit their jobs and started trading full time, but they're not quite making enough to get by. I also hear from retirees who want to supplement their meager retirement income through the stock market. So many people have so many different stories, and I get to help them achieve the success they seek. Not only does that feel rewarding, but it's incredibly fun. I love watching the people I've helped finally succeed. Their win feels like my win.

Many of these people will never meet me face-to-face. They use my service or speak to me online, but I still get to know them. We talk every day, and I find out about their lives, their hopes, their frustrations. Many of them have journeys similar to my own. Whoever you are, and whatever your story, I hope to help you, too, find success in the stock market.

TRANSPARENCY

Sometimes, people question my success. A common critique I hear is that the level of my success doesn't sound believable. "Have you really made that much money in such a short amount of time? If you're making that much money, why would you share your techniques with everyone else? Why wouldn't you keep it to yourself?"

These are fair questions, but here's my response. Yes, I've made a lot of money, but the stock market is so much bigger than people imagine. There is so much opportunity to make profit out there. My success is a drop in the bucket of what could be achieved. In the grand scheme of things, I've only made a modest amount of money. I have much room for growth.

As for sharing my techniques, it doesn't hurt me in any way. I don't have to sacrifice my own success in order to help others. I enjoy it. Plus, I only got to where I am because of the mentorship of other people. Smart, successful people shared their thoughts, experiences, and strategies with me. I took all of those things and made them work for me. I feel an obligation to pass this wisdom on. The stock market is big enough for all of us to find our niche and thrive.

Another critique I often hear is that I'm being dishonest about the size of my profits or the effectiveness of my strategies. I've done a lot to combat this criticism. First, I've released my tax returns and account statements to the public so people can see the numbers for themselves. Of course, I blur out my social security number and address, but all of my financial information is available for anyone to see.

I have nothing to hide. That's why I am transparent about my success and willing to share everything I've learned over the past five years. I learned a lot from the people who were older and more successful than me, and now I'm simply trying to give back. That's something my critics can't seem to understand.

A DIVERSE COMMUNITY

My strategies and techniques work in every industry and every niche in the stock market. Anyone can take what I teach and modify it to fit their specific needs and goals. I'm not precious with my strategies. Modifying and using what I teach doesn't hurt me in any way. In fact, that's exactly what I did with my mentors. I only adopted a part of what Jason Bond shared, integrating it into my own strategy in order to improve my results. You might choose to do the same with my techniques. In fact, that's what I hope you do. Take a principle, an idea, or an approach that I share and fit it into your own personal strategy for making money on the stock market.

There are so many avenues for making money in the stock market. I love it when someone takes the wisdom they've received and finds their own personal approach. It encourages me, and I'm sure it encourages others. That's one reason I created a big online community, so people can share and feel encouraged by all of the successes around them. Also, it helps to have thousands of people keeping an eye on the market every day. That helps the whole community.

Most of the people I teach get the hang of it over time and become experts themselves, and then they get to share their own experiences with me. In fact, some of them have brought things to my attention that I would not otherwise have seen. Some of the biggest wins I've ever had on the stock market have come about because a community member pointed me toward a specific company. Maybe they helped me understand a data point or analyze a chart differently. In the end, we're all helping each other to make more money.

You're only one person, after all. You can't watch everything. That's why I strongly recommend becoming part of a great community like ours, where you can get the support you need, share tips, and get information about all sorts of trades that you might not have otherwise considered.

We have people in our community from all sorts of backgrounds. They've worked in a wide variety of industries, from cosmetics to tech to oil, so there's a broad knowledge base to draw from. Within our community, we have a number of doctors, and their expertise has been a tremendous help. For example, we have one doctor who specializes in antibiotics. Since biotech is my primary niche, I occasionally approach him with questions about companies producing antibiotics, and he's always generous with his advice. Having access to such a diverse community helps everyone. We're all encouraging and sharing with one another, cheering each other on as we achieve our goals.

MAKING A DIFFERENCE IN THE WORLD

In every industry and every line of work, people are hoping to achieve some degree of success in life. Once you achieve that success, however you define it, you might want to take what you've achieved and use it to help others or make a positive difference in the world. I think that's true of most people. Most people dream about making some kind of change in the world, contributing to a cause, helping some suffering group of people. Presently, your limited resources might hinder how much you can do for others. For example, maybe you would love to volunteer at the local homeless shelter, but you just can't do it consistently because of the demands of your regular job. Maybe you want to donate to cancer research, but after paying all of your bills, you just don't have much to contribute.

With trading, you can finally free up enough time and accrue enough money to give to the causes that are important to you. For me, it has allowed me to connect with thousands of people online and affect their lives in a positive way.

One of those people was a family man named Peter. He has been using my services since day one, when I launched my online platform almost two years ago. Just recently, Peter messaged me and told me he had quit his job to start working from home. His journey was similar to mine, and it made me incredibly happy to be able to provide some advice to help him realize his goal.

Alex is another individual who I've been able to help. Like me, he formerly worked in real estate, but he had quit his job, and he now uses my services to grow his account. I enjoy seeing him experience the same freedom and flexibility that I've achieved.

I get to help make a difference in people's lives. For example, I had a member who emailed me to tell me a stock he'd bought went up 50 percent in one night. He had family in India that he hadn't seen in years because he couldn't afford to visit them. However, with this sudden windfall, he was able to buy plane tickets for the whole family to come and visit him in America. After years of separation, the whole family was finally reunited. The techniques that I'd shared with him actually had a direct impact on his family. These kinds of stories bring me so much joy.

It's one thing to donate your time and money to positively affect your own life, but I hear stories all the time about people in my community contributing to causes around the world. They're giving to charitable organizations, medical research, and important social causes. All of that is possible because these individuals have mastered their niche in the stock market. If you will dedicate yourself to finding and mastering your own niche, you, too, can achieve a level of success that allows you to help yourself, your loved ones, and communities around the world.

Conclusion

Take my story as proof that you can take a small amount of money and turn it into a large amount in a very short period of time through a smart stock trading strategy. It doesn't happen overnight. This isn't like playing the lottery. You have to put in a lot of hard work and persevere through some tough challenges, but if you're dedicated and passionate, that shouldn't be a problem.

Even though success doesn't happen overnight, with the right strategy and enough hard work, it does come faster with stock trading that just about any other industry. I don't believe that my success is unique or unattainable by others, and I went from $15,000 in savings and $80,000 in debt to $3 million in a few years. However, with that incredible potential comes some big risks, so you have to learn your industry and perfect your strategy. There aren't many places that will teach you the ropes, and your lack of knowledge is the largest barrier in your way.

Because of a lack of resources, many people start from scratch, knowing very little if anything about successful stock trading. Fortunately, learning how to trade isn't particularly difficult, in my opinion. You can compensate for your lack of knowledge and experience with hard work and determination. I genuinely believe anyone can do this. You don't have to be a genius. You only need a computer and an internet connection, and you can figure out how to trade successfully.

Although there is competition in the market, ultimately, trading is more of a battle against yourself than anything else. You must learn to let go of your ego, embrace different strategies, tweak your approach, invest plenty of time to educate yourself, and take baby steps. If you'll ease in rather than dive headfirst in the beginning, you can make a lot of progress in the stock market in a decent amount of time.

For me, the recipe for success comes down to a few simple things: educate yourself, select a niche that you can become an expert in, and find a mentor or community to learn from. Your mentor can be someone you meet with face-to-face, or it can be someone you follow through books, podcasts, and online. This recipe can help you get started in stock trading and develop a business model that will produce major profits.

Your business model might ultimately encompass a range of trading strategies. Think of this as owning a corporation comprised of several smaller businesses, each one using a variation of the company strategy while still operating under a unified business model. Not every strategy will be equally as profitable, but working together, they will contribute to the growth of your account. As long as you stick with your plan and keep your emotions out of your trading decisions, you will go a long way in the stock market.

GET ANSWERS IN REAL TIME, ALL THE TIME

When you start to achieve success in the stock market, it feels incredibly empowering. Not only does it build your confidence, enabling you to strive for even greater success, but it's a whole lot of fun. Seeing your account grow is a thrill. Being able to help your family, friends, and charities you care about is also a thrill. You create a better life for yourself and make a difference in the world around you at the same time.

While sharing your wealth to help others is great, I think sharing the knowledge you acquire is even more valuable. Once you become an expert, you get to help other people start their journey. Like me, you'll be able to say, "I've been where you are now. It took me a while to figure out how to succeed in the stock market, and here is what I've learned. Maybe with my help, you can achieve the same kind of success a little bit faster than I did." In doing this, you get to help change the lives of other people in a long-lasting way. It's far more powerful than just cutting someone a check.

I continue to find new ways to share the knowledge I've acquired over the past five years so I can help more and more people. The culmination of this effort is my website, Biotech Breakouts. The name comes from my original trading niche and my past experience in the biotech industry. These days, I trade in a wide array of sectors, though biotech still has special meaning to me. After all, it helped me to get where I am today.

I trade on a daily basis, and I'm happy to share everything I've learned along the way. The most in-depth mentorship I offer is called Nucleus, a video chat room where I speak with members of my online community, answer questions, offer solutions, and stream my actual live trading screen all day. With Nucleus, I offer something I wish I'd had when I started trading. Even though I had a few mentors, both online and in real life, who answered questions for me from time to time, I never had access to mentors in real time all the time. That's what I am attempting to provide—the ability to pull up an online chair and sit right next to me. By doing so, I hope to give people a head start, helping them to get through the early stages of stock trading faster than I did.

FIND SUCCESS QUICKLY

Even though it took me five years to get to where I am today, people still view me as an overnight millionaire. My growth took a lot of time and hard work, and my goal now is to cut that timeframe down for others. Instead of taking five years to achieve this level of success, I'm convinced most people can go from knowing nothing about the stock market to becoming an expert and making good money within twelve to eighteen months. Once people learn these techniques and skillsets, it will serve them for a lifetime.

If you want more information about the techniques I've discussed in this book, check out my free webinar and e-book, which go into more detail. The webinar is forty-five minutes long, and the e-book is only fifty pages. The book you're reading right now is intended to provide clarity on the mindset you need to succeed in trading, but the webinar and free e-book provide specific details about the technical aspects of the stock market. Together, these three resources will give you everything you need to hit the ground running, so I strongly encourage you check them out.

All of my resources, including Nucleus and the free eBook

and webinar, can be found at my website, http://Biotech-Breakouts.com. Whatever your long-term hopes and goals are in stock trading, I want to help you get there, and I'm confident that you have the potential to achieve the kind of success you've dreamed about. A better life might be just around the corner.

About the Author

 **KYLE DENNIS** didn't have any special connections in the financial industry. He grew up in an average middle-class family in Los Angeles and graduated from UCLA. All he brought to the table were the values of hard work, dedication, and passion that he learned from his parents. Kyle is living proof that you don't have to be a genius to make the stock market work for you. You just have to apply yourself and persevere with the right strategy. Now, he enjoys helping others become successful traders through his website, Biotech Breakouts, and his Nucleus mentorship program.

Made in the USA
Coppell, TX
19 February 2020

15988535R00076